G L O R I A

NO DEPOSIT
NO RETURN

K E N N E T H
C O P E L A N D
P U B L I C A T I O N S

No Deposit—No Return

ISBN 0-88114-969-1   30-0534

10 09 08 07 06 05   10 9 8 7 6 5

Kenneth Copeland Publications
Fort Worth, Texas 76192-0001

For more information about Kenneth Copeland Ministries, call (800) 600-7395 or visit www.kcm.org.

NO DEPOSIT NO RETURN

How much do you have in your bank account today?

I know that is a personal question, but I'm not asking so you can write and tell me the answer. I'm asking because I want you to notice something. Without even opening your checkbook, you probably have a good idea what the balance is, don't you?

You may not know to the penny, or even to the dollar, but you know whether you have enough to buy a new car, or just enough to buy a hamburger. You probably won't make the mistake of trying to write a $20,000 check with only $20 in your account to back it up.

You're probably thinking, *Of course not, Gloria. A person would have to be dishonest to do such a thing!*

That may be so in the natural realm, but in the spirit realm, believers make that very mistake every day. The reason? They don't maintain a healthy balance in their spiritual checking account. So when they run into trouble and need to draw on the assets of heaven—prosperity, healing, miracles, etc.—they come up empty.

When that happens, most people think it's because God didn't want them to have those things. But they're wrong. God does want us to have those things. He sent Jesus to earth to defeat the devil so we *could* have them—and as far as God is concerned they're already ours.

Everything you could ever need is waiting for you in the realm of the spirit with your name on it. All you need to do is get it from there to here.

How do you do that? With faith.

Faith is the "currency" you use to transfer God's provision from the unseen realm of the spirit to this natural, earthly realm. Or, as Hebrews 11:1 says, "...faith is the substance of things hoped for, the evidence of things not seen."

Spiritual currency works in the same way as natural currency. If you have an abundance in your natural bank account, you can enjoy plenty of material things. If you have an abundance of faith in your spiritual account, you can enjoy plenty of *everything*—wealth, health, good relation-ships, peace, success—because the Bible says God "...giveth us richly all things to enjoy" (1 Timothy 6:17).

Every Christian I've ever met thinks that faith is a good thing. They'll say, "Yes, sister, we all need to have faith." They'll even buy greeting cards with "Just Have Faith" poems on them to comfort each other in hard times.

The problem is, many of them have no

clue where faith actually comes from, where it's stored, or how to get it out when needed. That's crucial information. In fact, without it, you're spiritually broke. So, let's look at these questions one by one.

Where Does Faith Come From?

Romans 10:17 answers that question clearly: "Faith cometh by hearing, and hearing by the word of God."

Faith comes in response to the promises of God. Whatever God promises you in His Word, you can count on because He is "...alert and active, watching over [His] word to perform it" (Jeremiah 1:12, *The Amplified Bible*).

So if you want some faith, start by finding out what God has said. Open your Bible and discover what belongs to you according to His Word. Keep that Word in front of your eyes, in your ears and in your mouth. Proverbs 4:20-22 puts it this way: "My son, attend to my words; incline thine ear unto my sayings. Let them not depart from thine eyes; keep them in the midst of thine heart. For they are life unto those that find them, and health to all their flesh."

The word *attend* in that passage means "to pay close attention to something." The nurse attending a sick patient watches diligently over that patient. Faith comes when you give the same kind of diligence to the Word that God told Joshua to give it. When you let the Word of God "...not depart out of your mouth, but...meditate on it day and night, that you may observe and do according to all that is written in it. For then you shall make your way prosperous, and then you shall deal wisely and have good success" (Joshua 1:8, *The Amplified Bible*).

Where Is Faith Stored?

Now that we know where faith comes from, let's look at the second thing we need to know: Where is faith stored?

Some people make the mistake of thinking God stores faith in heaven with Him. So when they need it, they pray, "Oh God, please, give me more faith."

These prayers never work because faith isn't stored somewhere far away. It isn't in heaven. It isn't in the church building. It isn't even next door. Where is it? Let's look in the Bible and find out: "The word is nigh thee, even in thy mouth, and in thy heart: that is, the word of faith, which we preach.... For with the heart man believeth unto righteousness; and with the mouth confession is made unto salvation" (Romans 10:8, 10).

Faith is stored up in your heart—and since your faith (or lack of it) determines your future, the truth is, your future is stored up in your heart as well.

Think about that. Your future is stored up in your heart! It's not dictated by your history, or your current circumstances. Your future is determined by you.

Jesus said, "...out of the abundance of the heart the mouth speaketh. A good man out of the good treasure of the heart bringeth forth good things: and an evil man out of the evil treasure bringeth forth evil things" (Matthew 12:34-35).

Now, consider this: Who stored up the evil things in the evil man's heart? Obviously, the man himself did it. Who stored up the good things in the good man's heart? Again, the man himself did.

By the same token, you're the only one who can make deposits in your own heart. Your spouse can't do it for you. Your pastor can't do it for you. Even God can't do it for you.

God has already done His part. He made your heart to be a depository for His Word. He opened the account for you when you were a spiritual baby. As the Scripture says, "...God hath dealt to every man the measure of faith" (Romans 12:3). The moment you were born again, He put the initial measure of faith in your heart—but you're the only one who can make that measure increase.

As we've already established, you do that by putting the Word of God into your heart. Each time you make a Word deposit, your faith balance grows. Isn't that exciting?

Right now you may not be in a position to make huge deposits into your earthly bank account. But you can make any size deposit into your heart account. That's the account that really matters because it's the one you're going to draw from to change circumstances in your life. It holds the faith you'll need to cover any bill the devil tries to send your way. Or if he tries to put sickness and disease on you, that account holds faith from the Word of God about healing that will give you victory in that area.

But, remember, you can't make a withdrawal from an account that doesn't have anything in it. No deposit—no return!

Some people don't understand that. They see someone else getting their circumstances turned around by faith and think, *Well, faith worked for that person so I'll just do what he did and it will work for me too.*

That's not necessarily true. You may know someone who can write a check for a million dollars, but that doesn't mean you can. It depends on whether you've deposited that much money in your bank account.

Do you need more faith in your heart account? Well, put some in there! You can have as much as you want. Faith comes by hearing the Word. How much Word you put in your heart determines how much faith you'll have.

It's up to you. No one else can make that deposit for you. But then, no one can keep you from making that deposit either. If you can get a Bible, you can make a deposit every day. In fact, you'd better make a deposit every day because chances are you'll need to make a withdrawal sometime during the day. And withdrawals without deposits can leave you stranded without sufficient spiritual resources to get the job done.

Making Withdrawals

OK. Let's assume you've been diligent to deposit the Word in your heart. Your account is full of faith. How do you draw on that faith? How do you bring it out of your heart and apply it to the situation you need to change?

You open your mouth and speak!

Remember the verse in Romans you read just a moment ago? It said, "The word is nigh thee, even in thy mouth, and in thy heart.... For with the heart man believeth unto righteousness; and with the mouth confession is made unto salvation" (Romans 10:8, 10).

When you want to make a withdrawal from your faith account, speak the Word of faith. Don't talk the circumstances. Don't "tell it the way it is." Speak the end result. Say what God says the outcome is going to be.

That's what God does. He "calleth those things which be not as though they were" (Romans 4:17). Before God created the world, He looked out there and saw darkness. But when He spoke, He didn't say, "My, it's dark out there." No, if He had done that, there would have been no change.

Instead, He spoke what He wanted to come to pass. He said, "LIGHT BE!" Sure enough, light was!

It's the same way in your life. If you want prosperity, stop talking about lack all the time. Like Charles Capps says,

"Don't call the dog if you want the cat." Talk the Word of God. Start calling yourself blessed and prosperous.

"But, Gloria, I'm not prosperous right now."

Well, just imitate God then and call things that are not as though they were! Use your words to write some checks on that faith account you've been building. You'll be amazed at what will happen.

Abraham, Moses, Joshua...and You!

When I first learned these truths about faith, I was thrilled. Back then, Ken and I didn't have anything but a big pile of debts and, in the natural realm, no way to pay them. So when I found out there was a supernatural answer, I didn't waste any time. I got busy in the Word!

In the years since, however, I've found not everyone responds with that kind of enthusiasm. Some people seem to want to float through life without putting out the effort to build up their spiritual accounts. They want to enjoy their heavenly blessings, but they don't want to develop the faith it takes to bring those blessings down to earth!

Don't be one of those people! Don't expect to get something from God without faith. It's not going to happen.

Abraham had to have faith to get Isaac. Moses had to have faith to get the Israelites to the Promised Land. Joshua had to have faith to get the walls of Jericho to come down. Rahab had to have faith to keep her part of the wall around Jericho from falling down. And if Abraham, Moses, Joshua and Rahab had to have faith, then you're going to have to have it too. That's just the way it is.

That's why the most important thing you have to do in this life is to keep your heart full of the Word of God—because everything else can be taken care of if that account is full. That's what Jesus meant when He said, "Seek ye first the kingdom of God, and his righteousness; and all these things shall be added unto you" (Matthew 6:33).

Whatever you do in life, whether you're a surgeon, a garbage collector or a school teacher, spending time with God and keeping your heart full of His Word is your No. 1 priority.

That's right. The most important thing you'll do each day is to make those faith deposits. Don't just make them in times of crisis, either. Make them *before* you need them. Go to Psalm 91 and proclaim your protection every day. Go to Psalm 103 and proclaim the things that belong to you by faith every day.

I remember a letter Ken and I received from a family whose child drowned in their swimming pool. When they came out and found that baby in the pool, he had stopped breathing and already turned blue.

But because they had made deposits of the Word of God before that time, the moment it happened they were ready. Nobody said, "Go get the Bible and look up a scripture." (Sometimes you don't have time to get your Bible. That's why you'd better get the Word in your heart. It will save your life.)

Immediately that family began to pray and rebuke death and command the spirit of that baby to come back. As a result, that child is alive and well today.

Let me ask you this: How much faith do you have in your heart account right now? Is it enough to handle a situation like that? Is it enough to produce victory every day of your life? If not, start making some big deposits.

Start speaking the Word day and night. Not just when you're praying or being spiritual, but all the time—at the office, at the dinner table, over your coffee break, even in your bedroom at night. Every word you say goes into your spiritual bank account, either on the debit side or the credit side.

Frankly, I think it's time we quit being so focused on our financial accounts and turned our attention to the account that's ultimately responsible for all the rest. We need to become spiritual tycoons, with hearts so full of faith that we foil the devil's every scheme.

If we'll do that, we will be able to buy back every piece of ground the devil has ever stolen from us. We can enjoy the riches of our inheritance at last!

Prayer for Salvation and Baptism in the Holy Spirit

Heavenly Father, I come to You in the Name of Jesus. Your Word says, "Whosoever shall call on the name of the Lord shall be saved" (Acts 2:21). I am calling on You. I pray and ask Jesus to come into my heart and be Lord over my life according to Romans 10:9-10: "If thou shalt confess with thy mouth the Lord Jesus, and shalt believe in thine heart that God hath raised him from the dead, thou shalt be saved. For with the heart man believeth unto righteousness; and with the mouth confession is made unto salvation." I do that now. I confess that Jesus is Lord, and I believe in my heart that God raised Him from the dead.

I am now reborn! I am a Christian—a child of Almighty God! I am saved! You also said in Your Word, "If ye then, being evil, know how to give good gifts unto your children: HOW MUCH MORE shall your heavenly Father give the Holy Spirit to them that ask him?" (Luke 11:13). I'm also asking You to fill me with the Holy Spirit. Holy Spirit, rise up within me as I praise God. I fully expect to speak with other tongues as You give me the utterance (Acts 2:4). In Jesus' Name. Amen!

Begin to praise God for filling you with the Holy Spirit. Speak those words and syllables you receive—not in your own language, but the language given to you by the Holy Spirit. You have to use your own voice. God will not force you to speak. Don't be concerned with how it sounds. It is a heavenly language!

Continue with the blessing God has given you and pray in the spirit every day.

You are a born-again, Spirit-filled believer. You'll never be the same!

Find a good church that boldly preaches God's Word and obeys it. Become a part of a church family who will love and care for you as you love and care for them.

We need to be connected to each other. It increases our strength in God. It's God's plan for us.

Make it a habit to watch the *Believer's Voice of Victory* television broadcast and become a doer of the Word, who is blessed in his doing (James 1:22-25).

About the Author

Gloria Copeland is a noted author and minister of the gospel whose teaching ministry is known throughout the world. Believers worldwide know her through Believers' Conventions, Victory Campaigns, magazine articles, teaching audios and videos, and the daily and Sunday *Believer's Voice of Victory* television broadcast, which she hosts with her husband, Kenneth Copeland. She is known for "Healing School," which she began teaching and hosting in 1979 at KCM meetings. Gloria delivers the Word of God and the keys to victorious Christian living to millions of people every year.

Gloria has written many books, including *God's Will for You, Walk With God, God's Will Is Prosperity, Hidden Treasures* and *To Know Him.* She has also co-authored several books with her husband, including *Family Promises, Healing Promises* and the best-selling daily devotionals, *From Faith to Faith* and *Pursuit of His Presence.*

She holds an honorary doctorate from Oral Roberts University. In 1994, Gloria was voted Christian Woman of the Year, an honor conferred on women whose example demonstrates outstanding Christian leadership. Gloria is also the co-founder and vice president of Kenneth Copeland Ministries in Fort Worth, Texas.

Learn more about Kenneth Copeland Ministries
by visiting our Web site at **www.kcm.org**

Materials to Help You Receive Your Healing
by Gloria Copeland

Books

* And Jesus Healed Them All
  God's Prescription for Divine Health
* Harvest of Health
  Words That Heal (gift book with CD enclosed)

Audio Resources

God Is a Good God
God Wants You Well
Healing School
Be Made Whole—Live Long, Live Healthy

Video Resources

Healing School: God Wants You Well
Know Him as Healer
Be Made Whole—Live Long, Live Healthy

DVD Resources

Be Made Whole—Live Long, Live Healthy

Books Available From
Kenneth Copeland Ministries

by Kenneth Copeland

* A Ceremony of Marriage
  A Matter of Choice
  Covenant of Blood
  Faith and Patience—The Power Twins
* Freedom From Fear
  Giving and Receiving
  Honor—Walking in Honesty, Truth and Integrity
  How to Conquer Strife
  How to Discipline Your Flesh
  How to Receive Communion
  In Love There Is No Fear
  Know Your Enemy
  Living at the End of Time—
      A Time of Supernatural Increase
  Love Never Fails
  Mercy—The Divine Rescue of the Human Race
* Now Are We in Christ Jesus
  One Nation Under God (gift book with CD enclosed)
* Our Covenant With God
  Partnership, Sharing the Vision—Sharing the Grace
* Prayer—Your Foundation for Success
* Prosperity: The Choice Is Yours
  Rumors of War
* Sensitivity of Heart
* Six Steps to Excellence in Ministry
* Sorrow Not! Winning Over Grief and Sorrow
* The Decision Is Yours
* The Force of Faith
* The Force of Righteousness

*Available in Spanish

by Gloria Copeland

Pleasing the Father

Pressing In—It's Worth It All

Shine On!

The Grace That Makes Us Holy

The Power to Live a New Life

The Protection of Angels

There Is No High Like the Most High

The Secret Place of God's Protection
    (gift book with CD enclosed)

The Unbeatable Spirit of Faith

This Same Jesus

To Know Him

Walk With God

Well Worth the Wait

Words That Heal (gift book with CD enclosed)

Your Promise of Protection—The Power of the 91st Psalm

Books Co-Authored by Kenneth and Gloria Copeland

Family Promises

Healing Promises

Prosperity Promises

Protection Promises

* From Faith to Faith—A Daily Guide to Victory

From Faith to Faith—A Perpetual Calendar

One Word From God Can Change Your Life

One Word From God Series:
• One Word From God Can Change Your Destiny
• One Word From God Can Change Your Family
• One Word From God Can Change Your Finances
• One Word From God Can Change Your Formula for Success
• One Word From God Can Change Your Health

*Available in Spanish

• One Word From God Can Change Your Nation
• One Word From God Can Change Your Prayer Life
• One Word From God Can Change Your Relationships

Load Up—A Youth Devotional
Over the Edge—A Youth Devotional
Pursuit of His Presence—A Daily Devotional
Pursuit of His Presence—A Perpetual Calendar
Raising Children Without Fear

Other Books Published by KCP

Real People. Real Needs. Real Victories.
    A book of testimonies to encourage your faith
John G. Lake—His Life, His Sermons, His
    Boldness of Faith
The Holiest of All by Andrew Murray
The New Testament in Modern Speech by
    Richard Francis Weymouth
The Rabbi From Burbank by Rabbi Isidor Zwirn
    and Bob Owen
Unchained! by Mac Gober

Products Designed for Today's Children and Youth

And Jesus Healed Them All (confession book and CD gift package)
Baby Praise Board Book
Baby Praise Christmas Board Book
Noah's Ark Coloring Book
The Best of *Shout!* Adventure Comics
The *Shout!* Giant Flip Coloring Book
The *Shout!* Joke Book
The *Shout!* Super-Activity Book
Wichita Slim's Campfire Stories

_Commander Kellie and the Superkids__{SM} Books:

The _SWORD_ Adventure Book
_Commander Kellie and the Superkids__{SM}
    Solve-It-Yourself Mysteries
_Commander Kellie and the Superkids__{SM} Adventure Series:
    Middle Grade Novels by Christopher P.N. Maselli:

World Offices
Kenneth Copeland Ministries

For more information about KCM and a free
catalog, please write the office nearest you:

Kenneth Copeland Ministries
Fort Worth, Texas 76192-0001

Kenneth Copeland
Locked Bag 2600
Mansfield Delivery Centre
QUEENSLAND 4122
AUSTRALIA

Kenneth Copeland
Post Office Box 15
BATH
BA1 3XN
U.K.

Kenneth Copeland
Private Bag X 909
FONTAINEBLEAU
2032
REPUBLIC OF
SOUTH AFRICA

Kenneth Copeland
PO Box 3111 STN LCD 1
Langley BC V3A 4R3
CANADA

Kenneth Copeland Ministries
Post Office Box 84
L'VIV 79000
UKRAINE

We're Here for You!

Believer's Voice of Victory Television Broadcast

Join Kenneth and Gloria Copeland and the *Believer's Voice of Victory* broadcasts Monday through Friday and on Sunday each week, and learn how faith in God's Word can take your life from ordinary to extraordinary. This teaching from God's Word is designed to get you where you want to be—*on top!*

You can catch the *Believer's Voice of Victory* broadcast on your local, cable or satellite channels.

Check your local listings for times and stations in your area.

Believer's Voice of Victory Magazine

Enjoy inspired teaching and encouragement from Kenneth and Gloria Copeland and guest ministers each month in the *Believer's Voice of Victory* magazine. Also included are real-life testimonies of God's miraculous power and divine intervention in the lives of people just like you!

It's more than just a magazine—it's a ministry.

To receive a FREE subscription to *Believer's Voice of Victory,* write to:

Kenneth Copeland Ministries
Fort Worth, Texas 76192-0001
Or call:
(800) 600-7395
(7 a.m.-5 p.m. CT)
Or visit our Web site at:
www.kcm.org

If you are writing from outside the U.S., please contact the KCM office nearest you. Addresses for all Kenneth Copeland Ministries offices are listed on the previous pages.